Hope
in the
Valley
of tears

GOD'S
GRACE IN
GRIEVING
FOR
A MATE
By Valda
Peterman

If you would like your own personal copy of this book please call Valda Vi Peterman (269) 657-7507

Celtic Cross Publishing
Portage, Michigan

For information, contact us at: Celtic Cross Communications, PO Box 1207, Portage, Michigan 49081, or visit us at www.celticcrosscommunications.com

First Edition
ISBN 0-9740981-4-0
relationships/family

Dedication

To the loving memory of my husband Harm, who has taken the exciting ride to heaven on the white horse with Jesus. We loved so deeply; and to our two wonderful, thoughtful daughters, Julie and Cheryl, who never wavered in their care of me in spite of their own deep pain. I love you.

For my Lord and Savior, Jesus Christ. Thank You, God, for vision, strength, purpose, and grace. You alone could do it, Lord—in me and through me. I love you.

Acknowledgments

Special thanks to my dear friends Nancy Dorner and Carol Lacey for their invaluable help in bringing this book into being and to Erin Brown Conroy for her work with the final manuscript.

Cover Photo

The cover photo, taken by the author,
is the author's backyard view mentioned among the
pages of Hope in the Valley of Tears—first given as a vision of
the future, now living in the beauty of the present.
"I know the thoughts that I think toward you,"
says the Lord."Thoughts of peace and not of evil,
to give you a future and a hope."
Jeremiah 29:11

Contents

Introduction

*For your Maker is your husband—the Lord
Almighty is his name—the Holy One of Israel
is your Redeemer; he is called the God of all the
earth.*

—Isaiah 54:5

Countless men and women have become members of a "club" to which they never sought membership. It's called The Widows and Widowers Club.

I'm one of those members.

Members in the club recognize other members instantaneously. Some are new to the club; some have been in the club for a while. Many are strong, brave, and proud, willing to relive their own pain to help you through yours. They know the right questions to ask, have the real answers, and don't let you get away with "I'm fine" when they ask how you are. All of us find ourselves facing a depth of grief we didn't know existed.

This book is my story of grief. It's my personal journal, an accounting of God's grace while grieving for my mate. My husband's death was the hardest thing I've ever experienced; so great was my pain, I wanted only to die and be with him. But God had other plans. I experienced God's faithfulness daily, carrying me until I was strong enough to walk, strong enough to go on.

Even though writing down these immense feelings of grief was a struggle, I felt compelled to write "my story." My deepest hope is that sharing my story encourages you. The seemingly endless tunnel is long and dark, but I promise you — there is an end. Through pain and into comfort, our God is faithful. There is hope in your valley of tears.

Chapter One
My Prayer

Out of the depths I cry to you O Lord;
O Lord, hear my voice, Let your ears be attentive
to my cry for mercy.
—Psalm 130:1-2

Wrap Your arms around me Father… Please Father, I beg you. I turn to You in my grief. My love, the love of my life is gone—gone! I'm in shock. I'm dazed, and so, so lost. I don't know how I will go on, or even if I want to. I wail in agony. I beg for mercy. This hurts beyond hurt; oh God, how it hurts. Take my pain! Fill me; fill me, Father, with strength. Enfold me in Your grace.

As you begin reading
Hope in the Valley of Tears,
what is your prayer?

Chapter Two
The Shock

All the days ordained for me were written in Your
book before one of them came to be.
—Psalm 139:16

I finished frying the salmon for my husband's lunch and opened the door from the house to the garage to get him. My thoughts were on what I was going to say to him when I looked down.

"Oh! Here you are, Harm." My brain didn't comprehend what my eyes took in. There Harm lay, at my feet. Suddenly, panic filled me as I realized he shouldn't be there. He wasn't moving.

One look at Harm's gray face, and fear engulfed me. I knew he was gone. His silence crushed every fiber of my being. I ran my finger down his cool cheek. "Oh, Harm, no!" I groaned, protesting his death.

The lingering smell of fish made me sick as I ran for the phone screaming, "Father! God! Help!" In shock, I didn't know what to do, how to even dial for help. I dialed 119 instead of 911, reaching nobody. I threw the phone down to the floor and ran screaming back to Harm. My mind spun, confused, swirling, not clear. I thought, "Harm will tell me what to do!"

Groaning in agony, my eyes searched for some kind of life in his strangely still body. He couldn't be gone! I ran back for a different phone, tried dialing 911 again, and again misdialed. Frantic, I pressed the numbers to call my daughter. Her answering machine's drone spoke empty words into my ear.

Confused, I blamed the phone. Throwing it over my shoulder, I ran and grabbed the portable phone in my office. Desperately praying, I ran back to my husband. Harm still hadn't moved. Whimpering, I forced myself to look away and be calm. Taking a deep breath, I begged God to dial for me. Very slowly, I dialed 9-1-1. I was shocked when someone answered.

The next hours were a blur. Neighbors came. Family and friends were summoned. Our pastor and his wife rushed to the hospital to be by my side.

I was so emotionally shattered that a nurse kept track of my blood pressure, which stayed extremely high. The doctors and nurses urged me to admit myself into the hospital. Unthinkable! I experienced burning in my chest. I finally allowed the hospital staff to call my doctor for a prescription for nitroglycerin. The nitro didn't help. I didn't care.

It seemed like an eternity before the doctor came into the waiting room to talk with me. As I was told what I already knew, what I can only describe as a comforting feeling of love that could only come from God filled my soul. Truth sank down into the fibers of my being. Harm had left me. He had gone to be with the Lord.

Spiritually cradled in my Savior's arms, I crumbled. God's tears mingled with mine. I felt God ever so gently speak within me, filling my spirit with Psalm 139— a reminder that all of my days are ordained by a Sovereign God. Even this one.

The familiar words brought me great comfort. The words assured me that, even in the, thick pain, God was still in control. God was asking me to trust Him.

Knowing Harm was safe in the hands of God, my quivering lips kissed my darling mate of 43 years goodbye.

We are all but a step away from eternity, Father. Thank You, that You are sovereign and in control, that You are the Shepherd and Overseer of my soul.

God is in control in my life
in these ways:

Chapter Three
Angels Assist Me

"See, I am sending an angel ahead of you to guard you along the way and to bring you to the place I have prepared."
—Exodus 23:20

On the way home from the hospital, everyone and everything moved in slow motion. I still don't remember who drove me home. Locked in a bubble of pain and surrealism, silence surrounded me. A strange feeling overwhelmed me. It was if the car shifted into a setting called "peace" and we were floating, as if suspended on a cloud. Once, I looked behind us. The pastor and his wife led a convoy of familiar looking vehicles. It was much too much effort to try to figure out whose cars they were.

Our car passed people nonchalantly working in their yards. Why did they act like nothing had happened? Didn't they know that Harm was gone? When we turned into my driveway, the flowers Harm had planted never looked more beautiful. Each waving blossom stood out in brilliant three dimensional color. As I stepped from the car, the aroma pressed into the air around me in sugary perfume.

Disbelief kept returning: My bright-eyed Harm, always so vitally active, was gone. I wrestled with the feeling of needing to turn around and go back to the hospital for him; but the whispers of angels placed strength into my steps. "Hold your head up high! Move forward! You're a child of God! He will prepare the way ahead for you." Tears flowed again. Deep inside my mind and emotions, I knew the God of the universe who cared for me was encouraging me, speaking to me. I knew that the days ahead would not be easy. I prayed for God's loving grace to carry me.

Father, what You are asking of me is so hard. I hold on to King David's example in the book of Second Samuel, when his son died. David said, "I will go to him, but he will not return to me." He knew that his son was gone, but, in faith, King David also went on with his life. Fill me, my Lord, with that kind of faith—faith to go on.

My prayer today is:

Chapter Four
My Letter

"Deep calls to deep in the roar of your waterfalls;
all your waves and breakers have swept over me"
—Psalm 42:7

Night fell. I lay too wounded to sleep. After all was quiet, I got back up and wrote a letter to my Harm. I curled my body deep into Harm's favorite chair, embracing his lingering scent. My hand trembled. Deep, agonizing sobs melted me as I said goodbye to the love of my life.

> My Darling Husband,
> Today, when I found you "sleeping in Christ" next to the back door, my heart stopped. I was so afraid, Harm. I wanted to go with you. I didn't want to be left behind. I knew my life would never be the same.
> The magic we had together is gone.
> A part of me will forever be with you. You hold that part of me until I come. Oh, Harm—How will I be able to go on? Our daughters are hurting so badly. My heart cries for them. The grandchildren are lost, too. They walk around in a daze.
> I look at all we did here together, and I know I won't ever be able to leave this home. It's all I have left of you. You loved it so much…so much more than I ever did. I'm sorry for that. You built me such a beautiful house. Thank you. You gave me

two wonderful daughters. Thank you, my love.

I'll forever hold on to the forty-three years we had together. We trusted each other, loved deeply, and always needed to be together. I thought I would be the first one to go. If I could give you my life, I would.

I have to give you to God now, Harm. He's asking me to do that. I'll miss you so. I don't know what my tomorrows will bring. It will be a walk of faith.

There are still so many things left unsaid to you. The words burn within me, words that I know will be spoken to you, once we are together again.

Go in peace my love. My heart is with you. When my work is finished here, I'll dance back into your arms. We will spend eternity together with God and all our loved ones. Until then, sweet peace.

Your wife,
Valda

Oh Father, my dreams have all been scattered like bird seed. How I dread the pain that I know I'll face tomorrow. To plan my own husband's funeral is overwhelming. I'm at Your mercy, Lord. Come, be my guiding light. Help me to plan the funeral in such a way it brings comfort to those saying goodbye with me to my darling Harm.

My letter of goodbye:

Chapter Five
The Comfort of Children

Sons are a heritage from the LORD,
children a reward from him.
—Psalm 127:3

On the day of Harm's death, that phone call was a moment that shattered the lives of our two daughters. Numb with shock, my precious young women rushed to the hospital, praying their dad would be sitting in bed waiting for them. How painful it was for me to have to tell them that he was gone. Though their grief was overwhelming, their concern for me didn't waver.

In the days to come, both daughters and their families stayed with me. With their help, we made burial arrangements in accordance with my husband's wishes. For the celebration of his life, the girls and I lovingly picked flowers from his own flowerbeds. We gathered his gardening tools, still dirty, and stood them next to the flowers in a wooden box Harm had made. With care, the girls chose which family pictures to display.

As I watched my daughters, I realized the role they were taking on: They became my protectors, a shield. They came beside me when I needed their care the most. I never loved them so much! Without my mate, I felt as an abandoned child, alone. Crawling was all I could manage. Baby steps would be my next goal. Until then, my eldest daughter and her family stayed with me, showering me with love and care.

Thank You, Father, for the gift of children. Their support and deep love are a touch from the hand of Jesus. I will thank You for eternity for this grace.

*God, thank You for all the
people who love me:*

Chapter Six
The Celebration of Life

I will praise you, O Lord, with all my heart...
I will sing your praise.
—Psalm 138:1

Much to my surprise, the morning of Harm's celebration, I awoke calm. The girls felt the same peace. I knew it was the power of others' prayers.

When we walked into the church, the first thing my eyes focused on was the cherry wood box holding Harm's remains. It sat on a table in the front of the church. I blinked away tears. The box was positioned in the very same spot Harm and I had stood to repeat our wedding vows.

I walked up to the box and stood heavy in emotions. Harm had stood in this same place many times for prayer. He deeply loved God and always felt very much at home in our church.

I touched the cherry wood lovingly. With a kiss to the smooth surface, I placed a single red rose by its side. It was hard for me to turn away, but the thought kept returning: Other people were hurting, and I needed to comfort them. I quickly rearranged all the flowers and the pictures on the table until they looked just right. Swallowing hard, I forced back my tears and turned to hug the first person coming toward me from the crowd.

Over two hundred people came to celebrate Harm's life with us. Though my compassion went out to them all, the moment with Harm's mother broke my heart. Harm always admired his mother, and now, she was so brave. Looking into her eyes, I knew how much she was hurting inside from yet another moment of personal grief. Her last two years had not been easy without Harm's dad, Claus, after his long battle with cancer ended and he went home to be with the Lord. A month later, Harm's brother's wife slipped away from the same type of cancer. The overlapping pain broke her heart. Harm had recently spent a lot of time with his mother, as he finished putting in all of her yard flowers. Her mother's day gift—two rose bushes—became a comfort upon his death just a month later.

The service was incredible, wrapped in the feeling of the Lord's presence. Our pastor's comforting words flowed into the reading entitled, "From a Loved One in Heaven." A guitar played softly while a duet sang. Harm and I loved that song. Every time we sang the song as a congregation in church during praise and worship, Harm and I turned and sang the song to each other. Tears of deep emotion flowed throughout the church, as the words' sweetness were released:

He has fire in His eyes and a sword in His hand
And He's riding a white horse across this land
And He's calling out to you and me
"Will you ride with Me?"
We say "Yes, yes Lord, we will ride with You."

We will stand up and fight
We will ride with the armies of heaven
We'll be dressed in white, we'll be dressed in white
We say, "Yes, yes Lord, we will ride."
He has a crown on His head
He carries a scepter in His hand
And He's leading the armies across this land
And He's calling out to you and me
"Will you ride with me?"
We say" Yes, yes Lord, we will ride with You"

That fire in His eyes is his love for His bride
And He's longing that she be with him, right by his side
That fire in His eyes is His burning desire
That his bride be with him, right by his side
And He's calling out to us right now
"Will you ride with me?"
"Yes Lord, yes Lord, yes Lord, yes Lord."
　　　　　　　　　— "We Will Ride," by Andy Park

As we left the sanctuary, the sound of LeAnn Rimes' voice singing "Amazing Grace" warmly followed us. That song had been Harm's favorite.

The strong feeling of God's closeness and Harm's presence carried me for days. It was a feeling and understanding of God's real and powerful grace.

Thank You, God, for carrying me through this day. So many people told me they'd never experienced a service like it. Everyone felt so blessed, so comforted—Your presence was so real! What an answer to prayer. What a meaningful send off for my darling Harm. Praise to You, Holy One.

The Lord is carrying me
in these ways:

Chapter Seven
God Relates to My Anguish

Surely He took up our infirmities
and carried our sorrows.
—Isaiah 53:4

Those first days alone, I was an actor in a play. Each morning, I arrived on stage and watched myself perform. At night, I went to bed rehearsing expectations for the next day.

Death had visited me before. Four family members died the previous year, including my precious sister's death just four months before my mate. Her death left me the final survivor of my generation. Through my life I'd lost and grieved for my mother and father, six brothers, and nine other close family members; but none brought me the deep anguish I experienced now.

My husband had always been there for me. When I grieved through the wilderness of each previous death, Harm showered me with his love and God's love. In mind, emotion, and physical comfort, we were truly one. I particularly missed Harm's physical comfort. The urge to run until I found him was unbearable.

I never felt so alone, so lost, so hurt. Going on without Harm was the hardest thing God had ever asked me to do. I wasn't sure I could do it—or even if I wanted to.

I realized now that the numb state of shock experienced in grief is a part of God's mercy. He protects us until our minds and bodies adapt to our loss.

Thank You, Jesus, that You called yourself a "man of sorrows, and acquainted with grief." How thankful I am You can relate to our human anguish.

Lord, I want you to carry
my grief. Here are the things
that I feel anguish over:

Chapter Eight
Our Prayer

*Be joyful always; pray continually; give thanks
in all circumstances, for this is God's will for
you in Christ Jesus.*
—1 Thessalonians 5:6

For days after Harm died, every time I went somewhere, I felt an urgency to get back home. The feeling that Harm was waiting there for me was overpowering, even though I knew better. When I drove into the driveway, tears flowed. I couldn't turn back the clock.

I couldn't bargain with God. I was to give thanks to Him in all circumstances. How could I give thanks?

Just a month before Harm went to be with the Lord, paranoia gripped us both. The grief of losing so many close family members in such a short time span stirred up concern about losing each other. We suddenly wanted to pray together about our feelings and learn of the other's last wishes.

In our prayer, we thanked God that He had recorded the number of days ordained for us both, and for His wisdom in knowing which one to call home first. Harm prayed for God's grace to carry me, if he went first. As always, "Worthy is the Lamb. Worthy is the Lamb," is how Harm finished his prayer. Harm's words echoed strongly in my mind.

Now, as I rushed into the house, the visual picture of Harm kneeling in prayer calmed me. "Worthy is the Lamb. Worthy is the Lamb." I breathed in God's grace and held onto Harm's words. Suddenly, I considered a new perspective; a new thought washed over me. It was a blessing to be the one left behind, to spare my love the pain of the grief I felt.

Thank You, God, for Your love that washes over me as I praise You. Help me to find the way as I put my trust in You.

The new perspectives I'm gaining include:

Chapter Nine
Personal Possessions

There is a time to search and a time to give up,
a time to keep and a time to throw away.
—Ecclesiastes 3:6

One week passed. Now I had to do one of the hardest things I'd ever have to do: deal with my husband's personal belongings. His everyday things remained scattered throughout the house, as if he were still there. I couldn't stand it any longer. I needed to remove his things in order to go on.

As hard as it was, I spent hours placing things in brown cardboard boxes, tearfully packing clothes and gardening books. Then I hauled everything to the basement. Later, when I was stronger, I could find homes for his belongings. But not now.

As hard as I tried, I just couldn't pack some of his things away. I hung two of his favorite shirts among my blouses, where they still hang today. Two of his hats and one undershirt rest on the shelf in my closet, his fragrance lingering on the fabric. One dirty pair of his socks mingles in my sock drawer. At times, I wear one of his coats and one of his flannel shirts. His billfold still holds its contents; I keep it among my scarves and look at it often.

Within days, I wanted his clothes back in the closet. Somehow, I knew that would be wrong for me, and I fought the urge to bring them back upstairs. Instead, I took one of Harm's shirts to bed with me every night and plastered my bedroom walls with Harm's pictures.

And then there were my wedding rings. For a long time, I couldn't give those up. My finger felt naked without them. Yet, every time I looked at the diamonds, the feelings of grief became greater. Deep feelings of survival made me decide to put the rings away.

What should I do with his truck and car? It was the end of summer before I could deal with parting with them. Watching Harm's friend drive his truck down the driveway for the last time, I cried. When I later saw the truck at the county fairgrounds with a camper on it, I cried again. Harm and I were campers; that was why he bought the truck.

For a long time, I looked out my kitchen window and visualized Harm in his car, turning into the driveway. My husband always seemed to be in a hurry, a smile on his face, happy to be home. Now, I thought, he is home in heaven. God chose me to stay behind. I keep hearing the angels whispering to me: "Don't look back! Your life is not over. God will lead the way for you."

Lord, this new journey I'm on is so hard. I feel like I'm walking in a fog. Help me not to get lost. My eyes are fixed on You.

Lord, help me to deal with the
new journey You've placed
in front of me by:

Chapter Ten
Strength from Sharing

*The Lord himself goes before you and will be with
you; he will never leave you nor forsake you. Do
not be afraid; do not be discouraged.*
—Deuteronomy 31:8

I spent hours reading books written to console me through my
grief. Books helped, but I was unable to find the one story to
which I could relate. Going before me, God saw my need to con-
nect with someone; He brought a beautiful person across my path
with who I could share my grief—someone who had experienced
the same feelings of loss. In those first two months, my new friend
helped me more than she will ever know.

During that summer, my daughter and her family took me
camping to "keep my busy." I met Tracy one weekend at the
campground.

I poured out thoughts to Tracy that I'd kept inside—like the
fact that Harm died the day before my birthday and Father's Day,
and that I was unable to give him the cards and gifts that I'd
bought. I placed my birthday gift, a bench, next to the river behind our house. I often sat there, looking at the river, thinking of
my husband and missing him. Harm and I enjoyed being "river
rats" together; our favorite time was the salmon run in the fall.

Why did we only have six short years together in this beautiful setting? I wrestled with God's "times and seasons"; still, I questioned God's timing. I may not understand it, but I always returned to the knowledge that God doesn't make mistakes.

As I vented the frustration of these short years to Tracy, I
knew she understood, because her own story of loss was just as
wrenching. We became good friends over the summer.

Thank You, Father, for understanding my need for a special friend who could relate to my feelings. Tracy and I believe our mates know how much we miss them and love them. What a blessing to know they are with You. Thank You for the strength we gained from sharing our lives together.

Father, thank you
for these friends:

Chapter 11
God's Leading

*May he give you the desire of your heart
and make all your plans succeed.*
—Psalm 20:4

As days went on, I enjoyed walking around my property and drinking in the beauty of the many flowers my husband planted. As a hobby gardener, he put the flowers in every year. This year, Harm planted just before he died. The rose garden—my favorite place that overlooks the river—holds a special beauty of its own. The fragrance from the roses floats all the way up to my deck, enjoyed by all.

As a couple, we had talked about building our retirement home on the Paw Paw River. We were in church together the day we planned to look for land. While praising God, the most beautiful scenic view of a river popped into my head. The river twisted into a lazy "U" bending around thick woods. One end of the river tunneled through overlapping trees and the other end snaked off, curling around an island. I saw myself standing at the river's edge, looking beyond rushing water fighting to get over a log. Then I peered into the lush green of the forest. It was easy to imagine deer standing there. My expectation of living on a river doubled as my hand joined Harm's. The smile he returned warmed my heart.

We were like two excited kids as we left the church. Asking God to lead us to just the right place, we drove to land near the Paw Paw River. We couldn't find any of the properties listed in the newspaper; the river proved hard to follow, and we ended up lost. Spying a road that looked promising, we assumed it would take us to the river and tried it. We didn't see any water, but instead, found a beautiful piece of land for sale that wasn't among our listings. With two and a half acres of mowed lawn and a long central driveway, treetops stood tall as the gorgeous land's backdrop.

Following the driveway to its end, we found ourselves on top of a hill. There below us, the river stretched out in exactly the same beautiful view I had seen in church. Tears flowed in awe and gratitude. I know in my heart that we had become lost because our Lord wanted to lead us to this land. God didn't want us to miss his Will for us! What a God of grace!

Thank You, Father, for the freedom of being able to enjoy my home without the guilt that we may have missed Your leading. I'm thankful to You for the special gift You gave to Harm and me in designing and building our dream home. I will forever hold close to my heart the memories of time spent here together with my darling Harm.

Thank you, God, for giving me these special dreams and accomplishments that my Love and I had together:

Chapter 12
The Battle is God's

Resist the devil, and he will flee from you.
—James 4:7

I hate flashbacks. The replay of finding my husband dead on the garage floor haunted me. Could we have avoided his heart attack? Why didn't I find him sooner? Did he work too hard? The questions were unbearable. Then I wondered if I "shouldn't" be thinking about that moment so much, and I began to feel guilty about having flashbacks.

Scripture tells us that false guilt isn't from God. Flashbacks are normal. Flashbacks can't be ignored. So I learned to deal with them—God's way!

Talking about the flashbacks with my doctor helped tremendously. Friends and family members who really listened to my thoughts helped too. Their understanding became "a hug from God." Prayer, trusting God for answers (which He gave), and reading my Bible gave me great comfort. Eventually, I was able to look flashbacks square in the face and tell the guilt they produced, "Heave-ho — you're not from God!"

Thank You, Holy One, as I submit my battle to You, I'm reassured by Your word, the fight is Yours.

God, help me to deal with these memories and thoughts:

Chapter 13
An Answered Prayer

He reveals deep and hidden things.
—Daniel 2:22

I dreaded August 18. It would have been our forty-forth wedding anniversary. Never had I missed my mate more! Curled up in my easy chair, sipping ice water, my thoughts wandered back to that dreadful day and one question I couldn't give up...the one I pounded Heaven about: How long did my husband lie there before I found him? I couldn't live with not knowing. I cried to God for closure.

That dreaded day of his death, I awoke not feeling well. We had only shared a brief conversation together early in the morning. Running into each other in the kitchen, Harm seemed fine as he turned to go out to work in the yard. Eyes twinkling, he announced that yet another load of top dirt would arrive that day. Thinking that our yard already resembled a Thomas Kinkade painting, I went back to bed smiling; I knew he'd be busy, and I didn't have to worry about his pestering me. When I awoke, I felt much better, and decided to fix Harm's lunch.

As I thought back to the events of that morning, I wondered again: How long had Harm been there on the floor? The thought of his lying there while I lay sleeping was my worst nightmare!

As I pondered in my easy chair, I noticed that the ice cubes in my glass had melted. "What? Melted so soon?" I complained to myself. "It's only been minutes." Suddenly, a revelation hit me. "Ice cubes!" I exploded, jumping up. That morning, there were ice cubes floating in the glass of water Harm had left behind—three, to be exact. One was larger than the other two. For some reason, I had examined the ice cubes that morning as I set my husband's lunch next to the glass, just before I'd found him. "Oh, God; what are You trying to tell me?" I whispered.

I rose quickly from my easy chair and ran for more ice cubes, glad for the icemaker. The cubes would be the same size Harm had used. I filled the same glass he'd filled that morning with some water and added three ice cubes. Excitement mounted as I set the glass on the same table where it had set that morning. Turning on the timer for twenty minutes, I waited.

The ice cubes melted in eighteen. I filled the glass with ice and water repeatedly. Even with more ice and the house cooled to a lower temperature, the cubes melted within eighteen minutes. Harm had to have been in the house just minutes before I came into the kitchen. We had just missed each other! God had found a way to reveal that to me and answer my nagging questions. Humbled by God's mercy, I fell to my knees in thankfulness that God revealed a hidden piece of the puzzle. His grace met another one of my simple yet important needs.

Thank You, God, for showing me that You are able to do far more than all we ask or imagine. I will forever be grateful.

*God, these are the simple
yet important needs
that I take to You right now:*

Chapter Fourteen
My Fears

*For God did not give us a spirit of fear, but of
power,
of love, and of a sound mind.*
—2 Timothy 1:7

"No!" I cried, as thunder chased a streak of lightning through my bedroom. "It-it won't hurt us," I told Ginger, my new cocker spaniel sleeping next to me. She yelped in her puppy dream as I ducked from lightning resembling a giant octopus. "You're on your own, Ginger," I screamed, diving under the covers as one of the lightning's legs of light reached out for me.

This was my first thunderstorm without Harm. I've always been terribly afraid of thunderstorms.

I dared not move. The thunder roared in my chest—or was that my heart pounding? My tears ran down my cheeks. "Oh God," I whimpered. "It has been forever since I've felt this fear, and I'm so scared. Am I going to be able to make it without Harm?"

As a young girl, every storm was spent under the covers in fear. Surprised at my reactions to storms, Harm cleverly coaxed me out from beneath my fear. The years rolled back like the rumbling thunder as I recalled how he'd changed my perspective.

The first time we'd experienced a thunderstorm together, I automatically dove deep under the covers at the thunder's first clamor, leaving Harm dumbfounded. Looking back, I'm surprised that he didn't just throw back the covers and ask why I was in hiding. Instead, he crawled under the covers with me. His face close to mine, he asked, "What are you doing?"

"I'm hiding." I'd pulled myself into a tight ball.

"Why?" he asked softly.

The words barely came out. "I'm scared."

"Of the storm?"

"Yes."

Harm paused a moment, then said, "I'll hug you if you come out from beneath the covers."

"No," came my quick reply.

Harm didn't give up. He thought again, and then answered, "I'll hug you oh-so-tight; the storm won't hurt you."

I paused now, thinking. "Are you sure?"

"Yes." He sounded very calm.

"Okay, but it's got to be tight."

That was the beginning of Harm's hugging and playful teasing during storms. He quickly learned that he could say anything during a thunderstorm, while I was in my fear, and get away with it. Oh, did he have fun with his newfound power!

"Did you know that you have pointed ears and a funny looking nose?" His eyes twinkled as he laughingly slipped in, "By the way—tomorrow, I'm going to need a hundred dollars to buy a new fishing pole."

No matter what he came up with, my answer was the same. "Okay dear, hug me tighter."

Harm understood my fear of storms. I still deeply miss his hugging and teasing. With God's grace, in time, I conquered my fear. I learned to hold on to God's promises as tightly as I held on to Harm: "For God did not give us a spirit of fear, but of power, of love, and of a sound mind." (2 Timothy 1:7)

Thank You, God. Because of Your faithfulness to Your word, I walk in victory against fear. Praise be to You, Holy One.

What fears do I face today?

Chapter Fifteen
Loneliness

This is the day the Lord has made;
let us rejoice and be glad in it.
—Psalm 118:24

I woke up crying, my insides screaming in loneliness. Despite my protest, the tears flowed yet again. I hugged my husband's pillow, screaming at God. "This is too hard! The silence is deafening! I'm too lonely! It would be easier to die than to go on!"

Anger spent, I pulled myself out of bed and headed for the den and my easy chair. Ginger followed me into my favorite room, where I start each day in prayer.

It was November, and snow floated lazily down over the river behind the house. Ducks played and splashed in their morning bath. Blanketed in snow's fluffy covering, the woods behind the river rejoiced in its beauty. Reaching over to pet Ginger, I marveled at the scene.

Five months had passed since my husband's death, and it still felt like only yesterday. I pulled my Afghan over my shoulders and head, determined not to cry again. I needed to hold on to the truth that every day was a gift from God. I wanted—I needed—to trust God to fill my days with something more than pain and tears.

While I prayed, Ginger played at my feet with a squeaky toy. She growled, tugging at my Afghan with her teeth. Her toy had slipped under the blanket, and she was determined to get it back. Without emotion, I lost my covering so that Ginger could reach the toy. In the process, Ginger caught her hind foot in a loop of yarn.

Trying to shake her foot free, Ginger's antics turned the corners of my lips to a smile. Toy still in her mouth, Ginger's movements more animated with each second that passed, I laughed myself silly. When at last she shook her foot free, the triumphant pup proudly carried the prize to her chair—a twin to the one that I sat in…Harm's chair. After Harm died, Ginger was a gift. I thought about how much my husband would have loved this funny little dog so full of life. A special gift from God, Ginger's little surprises helped fill my empty days.

Thank You, God, for bringing Ginger into my life at a time when I needed a companion. A joy that could only come from the Creator springs from her. I'm hurting. I'm lonely. But I'm now at peace. Each day, it's a little easier to move ahead. Thank You.

These are the gifts in my life that I'm thankful for:

Chapter Sixteen
Time is Healing

My grace is sufficient for you, for my power
is made perfect in weakness.
—2 Corinthians12:9 a

It seems like I spend half my life on my knees repenting for one thing or another. Harm used to get a chuckle out of my time spent in repentance. Every time he caught me next to the bed on my knees, he would teasingly ask, "Okay, what great sin did you commit this time?" With deep conviction, I would sigh and say, "Why is it that the hardest lessons I have to learn are the ones that I thought I already knew?" With a smile and a shake of his head, he would invariably say, "When you find that one out, let me know."

I don't think there was a part of my life that I didn't share with Harm. We grew so close through our years of marriage; we reflected the phrase, "becoming one." I respected and reverenced my husband. At the same time, we shared a sense of humor toward one another that was playful and fun.

Time is healing. When kneeling next to the bed in prayer, and there is no Harm to tease me, I no longer beat myself up emotionally. Now I smile and remember the playfulness and love we had for each other. Our Father in heaven wants my memories to be joyful, not sad.

Holy One, I know there will be ups and downs as I walk through this valley of grieving. When I walk through a rough day, help me to remember, "Your grace is sufficient for me."

Time is healing in my life.
I see it, I feel it, in these ways:

Chapter Seventeen
Moving Out of My Comfort Zone

Those who hope in me will not be disappointed.
—Isaiah 49:23

On Thanksgiving Day, I missed my husband deeply. Memories of loved ones who no longer sat at the table were agonizing. Picturing each person gathered around a huge table in Heaven, I reminded myself that I was still on earth for a reason. God would give me new marching orders when I was ready. My focus must remain on Him. In the meantime, I realized that I needed to get out of my comfort zone and keep busy.

On the day of traditional shopping following Thanksgiving, I "shopped 'til I dropped"—literally. Exhausted, it put me in bed for a day! But the getting up and doing, and the time with my daughter, was worth it.

I'll always remember my daughter's face changing from a smile to a frown as the woman next to her in the coffee shop purred, "Did you know that a cup of eggnog cappuccino topped with whipped cream and chocolate sprinkles has four hundred calories?"

"What?" Julie's eyes peered alarmingly into her coffee cup. In a tense voice, she continued, "I've been drinking one of these a day, Mom!" I burst out laughing. She didn't drink much of her coffee, nor did I. What a priceless memory. Between my daughters and grandkids, that day brought many new memories to hold on to. Keeping busy proved to be fun. Making new memories became invaluable.

Yes, I'll "shop 'till I drop" again next year; I wouldn't miss it for anything.

Thank You, God, for helping me tackle my loneliness through busyness. It was only by Your grace I was able to get out of my comfort zone and hit the malls. I'm only sorry I didn't hear You tell me to wear more comfortable shoes!

In what areas do I need to move out of my comfort zone?

Chapter Eighteen
New Memories

There is a time for everything,
and a season for every activity under heaven.
—Ecclesiastes 3:1

The Christmas tree stood tall before me, decorated in Victorian style. The lights on the bottom lay heavy, and the angel, proudly placed on the top by my fourteen-year-old grandson, sat lopsided. My daughter and her family helped me decorate this year, creating more new memories.

Without the lace and angel hair, the tree was different from what I'd decorated in past years, and my grandson noticed. In fact, he was anything but happy. "Oh, no, Grandma, not flowers and birds! That's a sissy la-la' tree!" lamented Danny.

"Think of it as a new adventure with your grandma for this season," I laughed. "It will be a new memory for both of us."

Stepping back, I admired the beautiful artificial tree my husband and I bought two years ago. I was glad it was up. It gave me a comfortable feeling that all was right with my soul. Just as Christmas was the beginning for Christ, it could be a new beginning for me.

Thank You, Father, for new seasons and new memories. This time spent with my daughter and her family is proving to be quite an adventure. I love being called to dinner without having to fix it. Julie turned out to be a great cook—just like her mother!

How can I create beautiful new memories during the next holiday that's approaching?

Chapter Nineteen
Holiday Blues

My soul is weary with sorrow: strengthen me
according to your word.
—Psalm 119: 28

Soon it will be Christmas Day, and I've never felt so blue. I miss my husband greatly. Memories pop up when least expected, bringing tears I can't fight. Even the Christmas cactus is protesting Harm's death with few blooms this year.

That year, Michigan experienced one of its worst winters ever. Except for a very small trail of water moving through the ice, the river stood frozen. I'd called to be plowed out 10 times in three weeks, and more snow was coming. The furnace broke—twice. As of that particular morning, the microwave was history—what "great" timing.

With less income, bills were mounting. Money owed to my husband, with a promise to repay—forgotten. My health "iffy," I finally decided that I needed to visit the doctor. I could count the times on one hand that I'd traveled out of the home. And why didn't the phone ring like it used to? "I hope I'm not wearing my grief on my sleeve," I thought repeatedly.

Though most of the highways stood closed that night, a courage that could only come from God welled up in me to venture out. I'd been invited to dinner and a Christmas musical with dear friends, and I'd truly looked forward to this particular evening. Terrified of the awful weather, I climbed into the car and pulled out the drive. To my amazement, I found myself traveling on bare pavement on the roads. By God's grace, I traveled easily and enjoyed a delightful evening.

I wish I could say that after that experience, I bubbled with faith and sailed through challenging moments like a spiritual giant. I'm afraid that's not the way it was. What I can say is that I have never prayed more or depended more on God, each moment, each day. Perhaps that's what God wanted for me.

Lord, help me remember that nothing will happen in my life that we can't handle together.

Lord, help me to depend on You for:

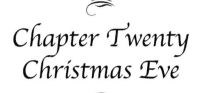

Chapter Twenty
Christmas Eve

*For God so loved the world that He gave His one
and only Son, that whoever believes in Him shall
not perish but have eternal life.*
—John 3:16

My prayer breathed in a sigh from my lips: *God, I can't believe tonight is Christmas Eve. I'm not sure what feelings will pop up as I spend this evening with my precious sister's family. We all miss her so much; the loss of my husband, their brother, weighs heavy on top of their grief. Our pain is yet so raw. Dance us through this night, Lord, as only You can. Twirl us until we're dizzy with laughter from loving memories. Make us eager to embrace 2001 with a new zest for life.*

The roads were particularly bad that Christmas Eve, so my niece, Karina, picked me up for a Candlelight Service close by. The touching service brought out feelings of missing our loved ones. Deep memories and emotions surfaced as we fought tears. Surprisingly, we knew many people there and their hugs became gifts from God.

Back at Karina's house, we enjoyed the family's traditional Christmas Eve dinner: egg salad sandwiches, a source of laughter in and of itself. Then Karina brought out some letters I'd sent my sister while she was in Florida one winter. Reading letters from nearly 20 years ago reminded me how close we were as a family. Memories of loved ones now gone jumped off the pages as we read. We laughed, we cried, we looked at old pictures and we took new ones.

Driving home that night, it felt as if love snowed from Heaven. "Happy birthday, Jesus," I whispered. God had heard my prayer.

Thank You, Father, for finding such a special way of allowing our departed loved ones to share the evening with us. We truly danced the night away!

*Lord, dance me through
the following memories with laughter:*

Chapter Twenty-One
Cherished Christmas Memories

*She will give birth to a son, and you are to give
him the name Jesus, because he will save his people
from their sins.*
—Matthew 1:21

My children and their families came home for Christmas and filled my heart with their love. But even with their love surrounding me, I couldn't get past that empty chair across the room and the laugh we could no longer hear. For me, the magic of Christmas was gone; my mind and heart kept taking side trips in memories, reliving Christmases when my husband had been with us.

One particularly dear Christmas filled my thoughts. The children were little, and we hadn't a lot of money that year, so I didn't expect a gift. When Harm surprised me with a beautiful soft-blue dress with an elegant slit up one side, my heart melted, and I'd cried in grateful love. Harm told me he'd used his hands to form my size for the clerk, and she'd guessed my size perfectly. Wearing that dress, I felt like a queen. I wore that beautiful blue dress until it wasn't fit for the rag box.

As my mind returned to the present-day, I felt such longing for the love of my life. Oh, how I missed my man dearly this Christmas.

Gifts were everywhere; I'd never received so many in one place at one time. All I could think of was how Harm loved gifts. I wanted to rush to heaven and share them with him. Emotions made it such a rough day; more than once I bit my lower lip to keep from crying, continually shooting arrow prayers to heaven for help.

My help came by way of my grandchildren. While in my bedroom filling my new billfold to keep busy, all four grandkids came into the room without saying a word. Taking turns, they each gave me a squeeze, then left as quietly as they came.

My husband deeply loved his grandchildren. Suddenly, each one of their hugs became a hug from him. Harm's love still lived in each of them. I held fast to those embraces. The day still wasn't easy, but it was better. God's grace came through in my grandchildren.

Thank You, God, for finding a way to bring me Harm's love. I needed to feel a hug from him so badly. You showed me how his love always reaches out through our children and their children. You truly are a God of compassion.

God, You're showing me Your love by:

Chapter Twenty-Two
Humbled

The righteous perish, and no one ponders it in his heart; devout men are taken away, and no one understands that the righteous are taken away to be spared from evil.
—Isaiah 57:1

The days following the holidays were a let down. As hard as Christmas had been, it had kept me busy. Now I had too much time to think. I thought about my sister, Mildred; I missed her so terribly. In February, it would be a year since we lost her to her long illness. Dementia at the end of her life humbled me.

Each of my visits to my sister were more heart wrenching than the one before, as she became more lost each day in her own world. I both dreaded and wanted to be with her. For eternity, I will be thankful that my sister never forgot who I was.

At times, Mildred's memories and clarity came back. In knowing, she'd tell me that she was dying, and we hugged and cried together. Other times, my sister invited me into her strange world. Those were the hardest times.

"Valda, come and see my castle. Isn't it beautiful? Look at all the red flowers!" Dragging me around the house, she "showed" me different scenes from within her. I wanted so badly to help her. Then one day, God opened up a door for me to walk into her fantasy world and, in a small way, understand.

For weeks, my sister believed herself to be living in one of our childhood neighbor's home. Not happy, she continually talked about her old house. I could see how badly she wanted to go home, but she didn't know how to get there. Everybody tried to convince my sister that she was already home—except for me.

Instead, I promised to move her back home, myself.

I often took my sister to the mall for ice cream. One day, before we left for the mall, I told Mildred that after our visit, I'd take her back to her real home. All the way to the mall and back, we talked about returning home.

As we got closer to my sister's house, I mustered up as much enthusiasm as I could and began pointing out familiar landmarks. I put everything I had into convincing her that we were returning home. By the time we pulled into the driveway, my sister sat up higher, checking out every bush, every corner with care.

"Look, Mildred! Isn't your house beautiful? Isn't it great to be back home? We should fill the pool this year! Remember all the fun we had at your parties?" Mildred's eyes grew larger, as I prayed, "God help my sister to see her house."

"Are my cats going to be there?" she asked.

"Yes! Bob [her husband] already brought them home."

"What about my clothes?" she questioned.

"Everything is here," I promised her.

Taking my sister into her house, I didn't stop chatting for one second. We walked through every room, opened every drawer, and looked at all of her things. When she saw the cat food in the cabinet, Mildred suddenly exclaimed merrily," I'm really back home! I'm here!" Looking at me intently, Sis spoke very clearly: "I don't ever want to go back to Dora's house again."

And she never did go back. That was the end of her mental traveling.

But illness sometimes doesn't let go. The challenges of dementia continued to deepen. Mildred never stopped walking; the calluses on her feet grew to the size of golf balls. Her body suffered and became weaker, as she never slept. To see my sister in such disrepair broke my heart, torturing me. I never felt so helpless.

Toward the end of my sister's life, I humbly helped feed, dress, and bathe her. Spending as much time with her as I could, I cherished each moment, knowing she would have done the same for me.

I always felt sad leaving my sister. Every time I walked out the door, I was humbled just a little bit more. It was as if I left a piece of myself behind with her that I could never get back. Once in the car, waves of helplessness washed over me. More than once, blinding tears forced me to pull over to the side of the road until I gained control of my emotions. In my sister's illness, my husband's arms comforted me; I don't know what I would have done if I couldn't have gone home to Harm. God's grace was given to me in my husband's comfort.

Three months before my sister died, we buried her son; she never knew it. As hard as it was to say goodbye to my darling sister, I rejoiced for her. All her suffering ended; she now resides with our Heavenly Father.

In my agony, I ask, "Why her? Why him?" Father, in Your word, You tell us that no one knows the day or hour that our life will end. We must be ready! Thank You for Your Son who died on the cross for our sins, so that when we die, we can be assured that we'll be with You. Thank you that we don't have to wonder whether we're "good enough" to go to heaven, for it's through Jesus' free gift and resurrection power we come to You and are made in right relationship with You. Come, be the Lord of our lives.

Father God, help me to appreciate these family relationships:

Chapter Twenty-Three
Special People

*A generous man will prosper; he who refreshes
others will himself be refreshed.*
—*Proverbs 11:25*

Seven painful months have passed. It doesn't seem possible that my husband has been gone that long. God has brought many people into my life, to walk through this wilderness of grief with me, and I'm thankful for every single person. I'm thankful for their prayers, for every phone call, and for every minute spent with me. Of all the people that have come alongside me, certain people stand out. These special individuals carry me in my grief.

My biggest blessing is that my daughter and her family stayed with me until I could handle being alone. I understand that, according to each person's circumstances, every griever is different in this respect. If forced to live alone at this point in my life, I'd be devastated. My daughter understood, and for eternity, I'm thankful to her.

Nancy, my dear friend and sister in the Lord, and Ken, her husband, encouraged me more than they will ever know. Filling my life with books, theater, and dinners in the finest restaurants, the time with them filled what could have been many lonely evenings. What a blessing!

Many people pray for me, but Sandi stands out as one who never stops praying. No matter how busy her life, she calls daily for an update on my needs. I feel her prayers; her friendship is a Godsend.

In an answer to prayer, one particular friendship has been restored since my husband's passing. It's an incredible blessing to have dear friends back in my life. The mending of the friendship is God's grace to me, and I'm sure that in heaven, my husband knows how God has cared for me through special people.

Thank You, Father, for reaching into my life and meeting my special needs through such thoughtful people. Lord, I bring before you those reading these words who may still be waiting for that phone call, for that thoughtful person to stop over. Perhaps they wait for a special friend to come into their life, an invitation to dinner, or an encouraging card. Help them to be aware of special friends as they come.

For different reasons, some are unable or unwilling to respond to those who reach out in care. I pray right now that each one feels Your love wash over them in waves. Allow hope to spring back into their spirits, Father, through someone special today.

Father God, I bring to You
my thoughts and feelings
on special friends:

Chapter Twenty-Four
A Poem

Those who walk uprightly enter into peace;
they find rest as they lie in death.
—Isaiah 57:2

It's hard to believe a new year has come. I was told that time would be a healer, and it's true; I don't feel quite as hopeless. The bad days are getting farther apart. By God's wonderful power, my life continues to gain hope. My mind wandered across the many ways God walked with me through the days, the months past.

I've been praying for some kind of closure to my husband's death; God found a way to bring me closure. I trusted God, and He didn't disappoint me.

When my sister died four months before my mate, I was devastated. Many people went through her long illness with me and sent me beautiful poems and readings. One poem, called "Safely Home," touched me deeply. I placed the poem carefully into one of my Bibles.

One day, as I read from that Bible, the pages fell open to hand me the poem. Reading it again, the words jumped off the page, alive in my spirit. Goose bumps covered me and familiar tears ran freely. Fresh realizations opened like tender new flower buds: God knew exactly what I needed and, over time, He was working in my life. Each question that arose in regards to my mate's death was answered. As I read the poem again, the words became my husband's words. Truth settled into my being with a new sense of peace: Harm hadn't died alone—God had been with Him.

"Safely Home"

I am home in Heaven, dear ones;
Oh, so happy and so bright!
There is perfect joy and beauty
In this everlasting light.

All the pain and grief is over
Every restless tossing passed;
I am now at peace forever,
Safely home in Heaven at last.

Did you wonder I so calmly
Trod the valley of the shade?
Oh! but Jesus' love illumined
Every dark and fearful glade.

And He came Himself to meet me
In that way so hard to tread;
And with Jesus' arm to lean on,
Could I have one doubt or dread?

Then you must not grieve so sorely,
For I love you dearly still:
Try to look beyond earth's shadows,
Pray to trust our Father's Will.

There is work still waiting for you,
So you must not idly stand;
Do it now, while life remaineth —
You shall rest in Jesus' land.

When that work is all completed,
He will gently call you Home:
Oh, the rapture of that meeting,
Oh, the joy to see you come!
— Priests of the Sacred Heart

Thank you, Lord, for bringing me these words of hope from heaven. I will no longer sorrow for what my mate has lost, but glory in what he has gained.

Father God, show me where I need closure in my grief:

Chapter Twenty-Five
God Opens Doors

And my God will meet all your needs according to His glorious riches in Christ Jesus.
—Philippians 4:19

My home-based business supports me financially. If I want my business to be successful, I absolutely must travel. Fatigue seemed to keep crawling after me; getting "over tired" was my worst enemy. As time for a business conference drew closer, I struggled with whether I should go or not. I knew I would miss my mate's traveling support.

It's always difficult dealing with my schedule at conferences, because I have a tendency to push myself to do too much. In the past, Harm protected me, making sure I rested. Could I handle this conference without him? Did I even want to? My excitement and passion for my business still hadn't come back. Wanting to know what's best—God's will—I prayed for answers.

"God, am I supposed to go to this conference?" Praying those words, I started to quiver; even the thought frightened me. My faith slid to my toes; my prayer weakened.

"Perhaps…if something exciting happened, I'd be motivated…" My head hung lower. "If not, that's okay, too," I added, hating myself for being so weak.

"I'll need a deep peace, too, God. If not, I'm not going!"

I stood up. There was no way I was going to find a peace in this, I thought. Rubbing my sore neck, I paced the floor. "Why did I purchase my ticket for my flight so far ahead?" I chastised myself. "Now I'm stuck with it."

I finally decided that this travel thing needed more prayer. The next day, I went to my friend Bobbi's house and spilled all. I confessed that I really wanted to go, but deep inside, I was scared. Bobbi prayed for me, reminding me fear didn't come from God.

The conference was only a week away. If He wanted me to be excited enough to get past this fear, God would have to act fast. Truth was, I still had no hope. So God surprised me.

That night, after praying with Bobbi, we held our weekly business meeting. On the way there, a new distributor rode with me to the meeting. I found myself asking the woman if she would be interested in going to the conference. Much to my surprise, she said yes. My heart jumped in my chest; I had to control myself to keep from screaming, I was that excited! I had no doubt that God stepped in.

The next day, God worked out more details. My sponsor planned on going to the conference, but every door closed on her ability to travel. I felt disappointed and concerned, for her support played a big part in my going. Then God stepped in. I watched in wonder as He slowly reopened every single door previously shut. The situation completely turned around; now she could go to the conference. Experiencing God's practical power was awesome.

By the end of the day, I could hardly wait to see what God had for me at the conference. If He worked out all these fears and details, He had to have something in store for me that was big! Before leaving, opposition danced in again, but with my faith back, I waltzed right through it.

Thank You, God, for Your strength that helps us to overcome our human weaknesses. I lifted this trip up to You as an offering of faith. I trust You every step of the way. Thank You that I can trust You in the middle of my weakness.

God, I give You these weaknesses and ask You to take me through them:

Chapter Twenty-Six
Angry at God

Answer me when I call to you, O my righteous
God. Give me relief from my distress; be merciful to
me and hear my prayer.
—Psalm 4:1

"No!" I spewed into the cold house, realizing the furnace must be broken again. Tears angrily pressed from my eyes and I slammed the back door hard behind me. "God! Can't you give me a break?" I cried. "First Julie and the kids get sick and go back to stay at their house. Now I'm all alone, and the furnace breaks—and right before I leave for the conference."

My angry outburst continued. "You know, God, I couldn't care less if I caught their virus. Can't You see that I need their support more than anything right now? Now, I'm not so sure I even want to go to that conference. All my courage is gone, God. Gone! Do You hear me? Where are You anyway?"

Sinking into my chair in disgust, I tossed frustrated words at the walls. "And now another problem with the furnace. I don't believe it! If Harm were here, he would know what to do." Suddenly, my body went limp, and I slipped into depression.

The night had not gone well at all. My nephew and his wife shared with me their plans for taking a trip, and it just so happened that their plans were identical to a trip my husband and I planned to take "some day." I cried all the way home. If I could have shifted my car into "fly," I would have flown to heaven and found Harm. God had had my husband long enough, and I told Him so.

In the chair, my thoughts thrashed within me. The longer I brooded, the angrier I became. I stood up and threw a book across the room, running to my bedroom. Passing my husband's picture, I stopped and looked at his image, then crumbled.

Many months had passed, and here I was feeling the same old feelings: How could my husband be gone? I pulled to my chest my big red stuffed bulldog that Harm had won for me at the fair. Seeing my sister's favorite teddy bear sitting next to where the bulldog sat, I grabbed that too. A gift to my sister from our niece, I remembered how Mildred took the teddy everywhere she went. That bear lay next to her at the nursing home when she died. I threw myself to the floor, and hugging the dog and teddy, I screamed in anguish at God: "Who can I call, God? You have them all! I'm all alone now. Is it fair that the only physical comfort I have is their stuffed animals?" I kicked, screamed, and cried until exhausted.

Laying on the floor, the emotion poured out from my soul, I spoke to God again. This time, my heart softened. "All right. All right. You're still my God. God, I'm sorry. I'm so, so sorry. Please forgive me for my anger, my words. But I hurt so, so badly, God. This grieving is too tough for me. Just when I think I'm okay, intolerable pain sneaks up on me, and I lose it again. Oh God, please be patient with me." Grief overwhelmed me; I cried until I vomited. Then I called my daughter.

My life hit bottom. I vented to my daughter until I had nothing else to say, and she cried with me. My daughter—my best friend.

We called and arranged to have the furnace fixed. The next day, my daughter and family came back to be with me. Though she was still sick, she realized my need for them to be there was more important than my possibly catching their illness. Somehow, I knew I wouldn't catch the virus, and by God's grace, I stayed well.

Thank You, Holy One, for understanding and still loving me as I searched for relief in my deep anguish. I don't understand why I had to lose the two people I loved so much, but I'm thankful that I know the One who does. Hold me close, God; don't let me go. Show me Your purpose for my life.

God, these feelings sometimes overwhelm me:

Chapter Twenty-Seven
Trust

I will trust and not be afraid. The Lord,
the Lord, is my strength and my song.
—Isaiah 12:2

It was the night before leaving for conference. I couldn't sleep. "What's wrong, God?" I whispered. "I don't believe I feel anxious. Why do I not sleep?" Only three hours of sleep later, I awoke to get ready to leave.

Still feeling I was supposed to go, I quoted a scripture: "I will trust and not be afraid. The Lord, the Lord is my strength and my song."

My traveling companion, Barbara, was a dear friend and business associate. We were a lot alike and always had fun together. Barbara's smile when I picked her up lifted my spirits, and I started to get excited.

Our flight was on time, but it took the crew forever to de-ice the plane, creating a late arrival in Detroit. With only a few minutes to make our connecting flight, we ran as fast as we could. I prayed all the way, asking God to hold the plane for us. At the connecting gate, the woman at the counter told us the flight was canceled. I told God He didn't have to go that far.

Then we hit another obstacle: The following flight to our final destination, Atlanta, was booked solid. The gal put us on stand-by, but made sure we understood there was little hope of getting on. So we booked the next flight, four hours later. We were not happy campers; arriving that late, we'd miss the biggest event of the conference. Should we go back home? It was tempting. Physically and spiritually exhausted, it appeared that nothing was turning out the way I had expected it to. As I prayed quietly to myself again, I felt surprisingly calm inside as God brought a thought to my mind.

I had heard somewhere that if you quit in the middle of a problem, the problem might never be solved. If I went back home now, I would always wonder if I could have attended this conference without Harm. If I trusted God, He would take me through these challenges, step by step. I knew I was supposed to go. Sighing in resolve, we sat down and waited for the flight. While waiting, we had the chance to talk to many people (whether we like it or not) for quite a long time, and much to my surprise, I actually picked up a business customer.

Eight hours later, we arrived at our hotel, only to be put in a room that obviously wasn't the nonsmoking room we'd requested. After a hassle with management, they finally moved the two of us—right next to my sponsor's room. Smiling, I realized that by God's grace, we actually had a better room. It was well after ten o'clock when we finally crawled into bed.

Father, thank You for delaying our flight to allow me the time to ponder going back home. Until I prayed, I didn't realize I needed those moments to truly decide that I would follow through with going, and that it was the absolute right thing to do. Faith that could only come from You filled my spirit, carrying me to Atlanta. Thank You for the business I picked up in the airport while waiting for our flight. I'll always remember it as a special blessing from You.

God, help me to see opportunity
and Your possibilities in these
problems and challenges:

Chapter Twenty-Eight
God's Strength

I can do everything through him
who gives me strength.
—Philippians 4:13

After struggling with sleep the night before, I was one thankful person when I slept eight hours the first night at conference. The day proved to be exciting: full of classes, very busy, and extremely fun. That evening, we ate a delicious dinner (different than any I had ever experienced), sipped dark coffee from thick mugs, and enjoyed a rich dessert. The day ended relaxed, watching TV until bedtime.

But when I lay down in the bed, again, I couldn't sleep. When a nerve pill didn't help, I started to feel frightened. Two out of three nights of little sleep wasn't good. I worried that fatigue might set in, and then, how would I handle that? At two o'clock in the morning, I was so upset that I woke up my friend. I needed to talk.

I didn't understand—What was I doing wrong? What was going on in me that I couldn't sleep? I had tried to balance my energy and make sure that I didn't get overtired. I had tried to be calm and relaxed. Yet here I was wide awake. I began blaming myself, which put me into a vicious circle of thoughts. I told Barb I would never put myself through this again. I read some verses to try to gain perspective. As a good listener, Barb's understanding and compassion allowed me to finally talk myself to sleep. I slept three hours.

In the past, a lack of sleep wiped me out for two days, but to my surprise, the next morning I was able to function. I knew God was doing something special, showing me how His strength could sustain me, no matter what. Barb had been His comfort to me in the middle of the night. I knew inside that God wanted me to learn to trust Him in good and bad travel experiences.

On our way home from the conference, the trip seemed much faster, and I felt great inside. Going to the conference alone took me to a new level of confidence, and I knew I would be able to go on more trips in the future. God's grace brought me through a challenge that I thought I couldn't conquer without my husband. By God's grace, I felt victory and strength.

Thank You, God, for holding off the frightening fatigue that would have kept me in bondage. Instead, You filled me with hope and faith. I felt Your promises being fulfilled as I was strengthened by Your power. Thank you for showing me that I can do all things through You, who gives me strength.

God, give me strength for these things:

Chapter Twenty-Nine
Home Sweet Home

*For I know the plans I have for you, declares the
Lord, plans to prosper you and not harm you,
plans to give you a hope and a future.*
—Jeremiah 29:11

Eight months after Harm's death, my daughter and her family
moved back to their home. We somehow knew it was God's timing, and when the decision was made, a peace flooded over us
all. Truly alone in the home for the first time, I roamed the rooms
like a lost puppy—and Ginger followed.

Looking out the windows at the huge yard overwhelmed me.
The yard had been Harm's world, and Julie's and the children's
world, while they lived here. Soon it would be spring, and the
yard would be mine. I knew so little about yard work. The rose
garden was the only thing I had helped Harm care for.

Flowers grew everywhere. The mowing and trimming of two
and a half acres stared me in the face. I worried about the large
deck; it needed to be power washed and sealed every summer.
Standing at the window, wringing my hands, I agonized over
whether or not I would be able to stay in this house Harm and I
built together.

"Oh God," I sighed. "How could I leave? This is my home.
You gave it to us. Our thankfulness to You is everywhere." Memories of our tributes to God while building the home surfaced,
bringing the all-too-familiar tears that wouldn't stop.

I thought back to the spring of 1994. As we built the house,
we continually recognized our home as a gift from God. Anoint-
ing a cross and asking Him to bless our home, we buried the
symbol of the Father and Jesus' love for us under the foundation.

We lovingly wrote a letter to God from the two of us and placed it into a wall. We wrote "Praise God" everywhere on the bare beams in thankful reminders of His gift in giving us our home. The contractor, a Christian, plastered over our bold lettering with smiles as he worked.

When the house was complete, Harm and I sat on the ground of our new estate bursting with joy as we overlooked the water. Hands clasped, we praised God. Our voices rang to heaven as we thanked and dedicated the land to Him.

I wanted more than anything to stay in our home—the home I loved. I felt close to God and Harm, safe in my familiar surroundings. Why was it that everybody encouraged me to move? I had heard it all: Scale down. Take the money and run. Get on with your life. Maybe they were right. Surely, God didn't want the estate to be a burden to me or to the girls.

For days, I pondered other people's words. The house suddenly became like a lodge; the two acres now looked like a golf course. Defeat washed over me. Believing I should move on, I told my daughters, Julie and Cheryl, my plans to sell. Both were saddened, but they understood.

God gave me no peace with my decision. Day and night, I wrestled with Him. In my mind, staying seemed impossible. In my spirit, I felt God leading me to stay. It made no sense. So I prayed.

Over and over, as my mind and heart prayed my thoughts to God, He filled my spirit with the phrase, "I will make a way where there is no way." When I went to church that Sunday, the pastor preached about the same thing: "I will make a way where there is no way." In the Bible study group that I attended, a song was sung that had the same words, the same message. Even some of the Christian books I was reading touched on the same theme: "I will make a way where there is no way." My eyes bugged out at each one of them. I kept seeing and hearing the same scripture verse in Jeremiah: "God has plans to give you a hope and a future." I finally stopped wrestling with God. God was not asking me to move. He was asking me to trust Him to stay. As soon as I turned my mind and heart to staying at the home, peace flooded my spirit.

I settled into my life in my home—yes, alone, but in my home, my gift from God. Soon, people began to offer their help in the upkeep of my beautiful estate.

As I sat writing in my office overlooking the river, a crane perched on a log and stretched its long neck into the water for a drink. Ripples drawn by a strong current glittered like diamonds. The sun winked at me from between passing clouds. All this beauty stood—and continues to stand—as Gods gift to me. By His grace, I enjoy His beauty in my home.

Thank You, God, for my home. I'm excited to see Your power working in my life. The offers of help that I've received so that I can stay in my home are coming from everywhere! Your grace and care for me is overwhelming.

Thank you, God, for these wonderful things about my home:

Chapter Thirty
A Bittersweet Memory

Then David and all the men with him took hold of
their clothes and tore them. They mourned and
wept and fasted till evening for Saul
and his son Jonathan.
—2 Samuel 1:11, 12a

Without my daughter's busy family around me, I quickly found
that the evening hours were hard to get through. Past memories
returned, washing a new wave of intense feelings of grief over
my soul. In my journal, I wrote, "Back to day one again. Will it
never end?"

One particular bittersweet memory followed me to bed every
night.

Harm was heavy into watching anything about fishing, news
programs, and documentaries—which I didn't enjoy. I liked to
watch old movies. We solved the problem by him watching TV
in the den and me watching movies in the bedroom. For a long
time, we communicated by hollering back and forth. One day,
Harm got smart; he called me from his private phone line in the
den. He had a good chuckle when I answered the phone and
exclaimed in surprise, "Where are you?!"

That was the beginning of our evening phone conversa-
tions—and the beginning of my pestering husband interrupting
every single movie that I watched. It got to the point where I
rolled my eyes to the ceiling whenever I heard the phone ring,
knowing it would be his voice. There was always something on
TV that he wanted me to see, and he'd talk and talk, trying to
convince me to change the channel. Eventually, I'd give in and
turn the channel to check it out.

But it didn't stop there. Harm continued to annoy me by calling me back on the phone every fifteen minutes for my opinion on the show. Well, I normally didn't stay on his channel; I'd only watch for a minute or two. That started a verbal battle of sorts. He couldn't understand why I didn't keep watching. I'd just keep saying to him, "I checked it out, but it wasn't interesting to me." Harm couldn't comprehend that I didn't like what he thought was great, and it drove him nuts. So he kept at me.

"How can you not be interested in learning more about your health, or about events happening in the world?" he invariably argued.

Many evenings, I took the phone off the hook just so I could watch my movie in peace. More than once he caught me. Suddenly, Harm would appear in the doorway, his hands on his hips and a frown across his face. "Just what I figured. Would you mind putting the phone back on the hook so I can talk to you without having to chase you down?"

He looked so comical, trying to be stern when he was really quite amused. Holding back a giggle, I'd put the phone back and promise him with a wry grin that I'd never do it again. We both knew I would. Many times, at this point, Harm would stay with me, or I would go with him to the den. It was a silly ritual, really. Secretly, I wanted to have his private line disconnected.

Sitting in my bedroom now, watching television, my mind came back to the present. I looked around the quiet home surrounding me. Tears formed as I glanced at my silent phone on the nightstand. I had his private phone line disconnected long ago; the wall is empty where his phone once hung. What I wouldn't give to have my phone ring, to hear his voice just one more time.

I understand, God, why David tore his clothes and mourned. I'm thankful to have that scripture to hold on to. It helps me in my time of sorrow.

Father, here are my memories;
help me to process through the pain:

Chapter Thirty-One
God has a Sense of Humor

Even in laughter the heart may ache,
and joy may end in grief.
—Proverbs 14:13

I sat in bed, munching on candy, searching for a good movie on TV, when Ginger jumped up, spilling the chocolate covered peanuts everywhere. We both fought for them, and my thoughts danced back in time to another night when chocolate covered peanuts had waltzed around on the bed.

My friend Barb and I were always going on diets—and failing. Deciding to try yet one more diet, Harm laughed when I told him we were at it again. With strong conviction, I promised him I would stick to the diet, or he could tattle to Barb on me.

That first day I did well—so well, I told Harm as I moseyed into the bedroom, "This is a piece of cake."

"Right!" he barked. "We'll talk again in a few days."

Chuckling, I flipped channels until I settled on a good movie. He'll see, I thought. There's no way I'm going to blow it.

Half way through the movie, I opened the drawer on my nightstand to get some gum, and there staring at me sat a bag of chocolate covered peanuts. "Darn! Wouldn't you know it, my favorite candy!" I cried, slamming the drawer shut. I had forgotten about buying them.

For the next half an hour I tried to forget what I'd seen, but it was no good. I fell into a full-fledged chocolate attack. I opened the drawer—just to look at them, of course. After thinking a moment, I decided to myself, "Two won't hurt." Popping them into my mouth, I glanced around the room like a criminal. All was clear. I quietly shut the drawer.

Fifteen minutes later I decided to peek at the candy again. I slowly opened the drawer and looked at them longingly. My mouth watered. Just one handful. That's all. I allowed myself a dip into the bag.

"What are you doing?" Harm said, strolling into the room.

"Nothing," I mumbled, swallowing the piece of candy in my mouth. With one quick movement, I slid the rest of the candy under the covers.

"Well, I'm going to bed," Harm announced, taking his shirt off.

"What!" I protested. "It's too early."

"Not when you're tired," he said, yawning.

My mouth dropped. Now what would I do? I'd slipped the candy onto his side of the bed. My only hope was to get him out of the room so I could retrieve it. I decided to give it my best shot.

"Did you shut off the TV in the den?"

"Yes."

"What about the lights?"

"Off," he said crawling into bed.

With fleeting whimsy, I started to pray in quiet desperation. But God has a sense of humor.

"What have we got here?" Harm sputtered, holding a chocolate covered peanut up for inspection. As he sat back up, more peanuts rolled across the bed toward him. Raking his hands across the bed, he corralled the chocolate beasts into a pile. With one eyebrow lifted, he looked at me and said, "Ah ha! Caught you red handed, I see." Try as he might, my husband couldn't hide the twinkle in his eye.

"I have no idea where they came from, Harm," I said innocently. "I wouldn't eat them if I were you; they might be too old."

He rolled his eyes to the ceiling in mock disgust. "You're pathetic. Let me look in your mouth. That will settle it"

I tried to get out of bed, but he was faster than me. Harm tickled me until I opened my mouth.

"Just as I thought: Guilty!" he announced. "I'm calling Barb, right now!"

"No! You can't! I'll do it in the morning. I promise. Just let me do it." I gave him my puppy-eyed look.

"What's in it for me?" He scowled, folding his arms.

"I'll be your cook and slave all day tomorrow—promise." I crossed my heart.

He smiled, slid under the covers and muttered, "I'll leave my menu on the counter top." Recalling this story, I laughed until a longing for Harm washed over me. Tears ripped down my cheeks as I sobbed. Ginger, seeing my distress, brought me her toy, and her distraction helped me tackle my suffering.

Thank You, Father, for Your sense of humor. You held that night in Your hands, returning it back to me when You knew I needed to laugh. My heart aches, but my joy is complete in You.

God, bring to mind the joyful times:

Chapter Thirty-Two
God Understands Our Weaknesses

My eyes grew weak as I looked to the heavens.
I am troubled; O Lord, come to my aid!
—Isaiah 38:14b

For months after my husband's death, I experienced burning in my chest, mostly when I was upset. I procrastinated making an appointment to see my cardiologist, knowing he would want me to have a stress test. How I hated that test! Harm called the machine "the harmless bike." I called it "Jaws."

Both Harm and I had had stress tests before. My husband had a field day teasing me each time he took me for a test. When my turn came, he would say with a twinkle, "Go get Jaws." I never let him know it, but his teasing helped. Without Harm, I didn't have the strength to face "Jaws"—or the results of the test.

To avoid going for a stress test, I decided to play doctor. Using an old lab order form I had lying around the house from having my lipid panel done, I went for blood work. I was sure that if my cholesterol came back in the normal range, "Jaws" wouldn't be necessary. I convinced myself that the burning sensation in my chest came from stress, not from my heart.

Before the results had a chance to come back, my blood pressure shot to the ceiling. "This is not good," I thought, as I took my blood pressure repeatedly during the next three days. I prayed it would go down on its own, but instead, it went up. My faith in my toes, I knew I would have to face going to the doctor, and perhaps "Jaws," without Harm.

Instead of a stress test, my cardiologist scheduled a catheterization procedure—in three days. As I drove home, tears tore down my face. Harm's absence pierced my heart. Never needing his comfort and support more, helplessness enveloped me.

O Lord, come to my aid! Why doesn't it end? Now what do I face? I'm scared! I'm weak! Every time I think I'm moving forward, the rug gets yanked from beneath me. Stop my spirit from trembling Lord. Help me get through this. Fill me with Your faith as I seek Your presence!

O Lord, come to my aid!

Chapter Thirty-Three
God of All

For your Maker is your husband—
the Lord Almighty is his name—the Holy One of
Israel is your Redeemer; he is called the
God of all the earth.
—Isaiah 54:5

To be without the person I most deeply loved—and who loved me—at this time in my life was unimaginable. I was afraid to go ahead with the testing without Harm by my side. I toyed with the idea of not telling my daughters about the test—and then canceling the appointment.

Years before, at the age of forty-five, I had experienced a nasty heart attack. Eighteen days in the hospital, Harm hardly left my side. My brother Lyle had such heaviness of heart over my condition, he cried all the time. I cherished Lyle's visits and my sister Mildred's calls from Florida—their support meant the world to me.

I had been in the hospital seventeen days when Lyle had a heart attack. We were exceptionally close. My precious brother— My best friend. My father figure, since losing my dad at the age of twelve. Lyle didn't make it.

Frightened to tell me, the hospital staff stood close by my heart monitor while they told me the news. Harm's words, chosen with care, remain etched in my memory.

The pain of the news of Lyle's death ripped through my body like a chain saw. Sobs tore at my heart. My pain mirrored in Harm's eyes, my husband held me close and steadied me with his love.

To survive the pain of Lyle's death, I pushed it to the back of my mind. Later, I experienced some problems as a result of shoving the pain so deeply inside. With God's help and Harm's support, I overcame the pain.

The following sixteen years were good years, a triumph in physical and emotional health. Harm's love held me at night; when I couldn't sleep, he listened to me talk myself tired. I shared my every thought with my husband, as he did with me. Hugs always started and ended our days. As partners, we could always count on each other to be there.

Now there wasn't anybody left in my generation to call. Lyle was gone. Mildred was gone. Harm was gone. Memories, pictures, and the terrible comfort of my tears were all I had. My heart cried, "Wait for me!" But they continued on their journey, and I on mine.

My faith, support, and hope could only come from God now. God was my husband. In Him, I had a future. If God is for me, who can be against me?

God, in my weakness I have come to You. In You, I have found my strength. I don't know what You have ahead for me, I only know I'm not afraid of it anymore.

God, be the Lord of my life
in all I do and in all I am.
I look to You to support me in these ways:

Chapter Thirty-Four
God is Our Healer

The Lord will sustain him on his sickbed and
restore him from his bed of illness.
—Psalm 41:3

Dark clouds gathered, matching my mood as I walked into the hospital with Julie for the catheterization procedure. Meeting us there, Cheryl and Karina's colossal smiles and hugs encouraged me. But it felt as if a herd of cattle stampeded in my empty stomach, reminding me why I wasn't allowed to eat and what lay ahead.

The waiting was the hardest part. It took six hours before the hospital staff could get to me. The girls kept me busy talking, but conversation didn't stop the nagging worry of what the doctors might find.

The test found blockage, and as I came out of the anesthetic, the doctors were putting in a second stent. My mind foggy, I listened as they talked. I could tell they were having difficulty placing it.

Troubled, I shot an arrow prayer to heaven. A moment later, the doctor said, "It's in!" and I quietly rejoiced. A day later, I went home. By God's grace, we made it through—God and me, together.

Thank You, God, for carrying me through a strenuous day. How thankful I am it's over, and that I don't have to go through open heart surgery. Please help me to fall in love with life again. I need to go on. Harm would want me to.

God, take care of me in these ways:

Chapter Thirty-Five
A Trial

*Consider it pure joy, my brothers, whenever you
face trials of many kinds.*
—James 1:2

I came home from the hospital with high hopes, determined not to baby myself and to get on with my life. Nevertheless, from day one, things didn't go well. I still suffered burning in my chest, and I found myself dragging from one chair to another. Convinced that I needed more time to heal, I said little to anybody. Instead, I tried to ignore my symptoms by playing a game of pretend.

I lapsed into a fantasy world. "Harm is on a fishing trip and won't be home for a few days," I told my dog. Cranking the music on high, I baked brownies for when he returned—just like I used to. Of course, the fantasy didn't do any good; I knew Harm would never come back. My chest still hurt. I trashed the food and cried.

"Okay," I thought next. "So I'm on my own. I can do this. I can feel good." Determined to make my life "work," I tried "running the roads," going out in the car and spending as much time away from home as I could. It was no good. Traveling around like a wild woman wasn't me. I'm a home person. And my chest still hurt.

"I know," I thought. "Deep prayer and Bible study. I'll pour myself into spiritual things." I was sure that would work, that my life would settle and that I'd feel better. But I was wrong again.

I tried escapism: "What about burying myself in my old movies?" I couldn't believe it—the old movies didn't work either. I used to love them. Now they were empty. And I still didn't feel good, physically and emotionally.

Giving up, I went to the doctor with my symptoms. I learned I had high blood pressure, which wasn't a surprise at all. Many questions later, the doctor's conclusion hit me hard: I suffered from depression. With a prescription for an antidepressant in my hand, I went home.

Fighting shortness of breath, insomnia, and irregular heartbeat, the next few weeks blurred together. I called my doctor and cardiologist so often that the receptionists and nurses recognized my voice. My symptoms worsened, and I had umpteen visits to both medical offices. The conclusion stayed the same: My symptoms came from the medications. I flitted from one antidepressant to another. I was a mess. Everybody was praying for me, but nothing changed. I stormed heaven, asking God to come to my aid.

God, You said in Your word, You would give strength to the weary. I am weary, God. What is happening to me? Why am I going through so many trials? Will it never end? The first year anniversary of Harm's death is coming. I'm ready to go on, Holy One. Please shut the mouth of hell and open the gates of heaven. Give me faith to walk beyond this mess.

Here are my challenges, Lord; I hand You depression and weariness:

Chapter Thirty-Six
God's Protection

As the heavens are higher than the earth, so are
my ways higher than your ways and my thoughts
than your thoughts.
—Isaiah 55:9

I refused to give in to depression. Instead, I focused on keeping up my yard. With or without sleep, I forced myself to work outdoors. I learned how to use the riding lawn mower, which, unfortunately, cost me big bucks when I accidentally ran into a fence. The service guy that picked up the mower for repairs shook his head sadly while I complained about reverse being in the wrong spot.

When mowing, my next problem to solve was how to keep the mower out of the river; that crazy river had a habit of sneaking up on me. I never told my daughters how close I came to using the lawn mower as a boat.

A steep hill finally convinced me to sell my John Deere. Taking one look at the incline, I decided the best strategy was to go straight up. I realized what a big mistake I'd made when the mower started rolling backwards. With wide eyes, I clung to the wheel and rode it out—until the wheels hit a big bump. As the lawn mower and I parted company, I knew I was in over my head. I decided to hire lawn care.

My next project was care of the flowers. Harm had a neat spot where he'd let all kinds of blooms grow wild for replanting. After I proudly replaced seventy-five dead mum plants in the front center circle of our drive, I came across some bizarre looking plants among the mix. When my daughter checked out the pretty transplants, she chuckled. I had replanted weeds.

Determined not to let the weed incident burst my bubble, I kept the pretty weeds and spread wild flower seeds into the rest of the empty beds. I figured that was safe enough. Well, I was wrong; the weeds choked out the flowers.

In spite of my keeping busy, I continued to fight depression. Many nights brought me to my knees in prayer. The only way I could deal with the pain in my life was to offer it up to God.

My shortness of breath grew worse, so the doctor ordered another stress test. To my surprise, I passed the test, and my doctor now blamed the breathing problem on arrhythmia—unsteady heartbeats—and scheduled an appointment with a cardiac specialist.

What's going on, God? Somehow I know You're protecting me, but I can't bring it together. You are in me; You know the silent pulsing of my blood. Please guide me in all truth; help me to understand what's happening, and keep me safe.

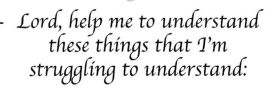

Lord, help me to understand these things that I'm struggling to understand:

Chapter Thirty-Seven
God, Are You There?

*Answer me, O Lord, out of the goodness of your
love; in your great mercy turn to me.*
—Psalm 69:16

Sighing, I looked out the window. The dreary and lifeless day matched my feelings. Again, I hadn't slept. "Why am I such a mess?" I whispered to God. "I don't understand. Where are You? I pray and pray. Everyone is praying for me, and still You are silent."

My body felt weak as I paced the floor quoting verses from the Bible that held special meaning. In spite of my efforts to stay upbeat, depression washed over me. My soul struggled against the feelings, refusing to give in to them, battling valiantly. I needed to plant more flowers, so I once again stepped outdoors to prepare a flowerbed. Working hard, I suddenly realized how hard I was breathing and how exhausted my body felt.

Looking up to heaven, I cried, "Not again! This can't be happening to me! Why, God? Why is this happening to me? They just changed my medication...I should feel better than this!" As I protested, rain burst from a cloud and intermingled with my tears. Becoming drenched under the gray sky, I hugged myself in the dirt and rocked back and forth, feeling utterly abandoned by God.

The rain fell steady now. "Okay, God! If that's the way You want it, so be it. I'm going to keep working!" Choking on my words, I pushed my dirty fingers into the now-muddy soil. Weak and frightened, I dug as hard as I could, screaming at God: "If You want to take me home, go ahead! Here I am! My life is in Your hands—take it! I won't call the doctor again! Those doctors are doing nothing, absolutely nothing for me. Nothing! Do You hear me?"

My hands pushed and dug until I collapsed. My face fell in the mud; the smell of the earth seeped deep into my nostrils, and I cried because I was still alive.

God and I talked for a long time. By the time I walked back into the house, I knew it didn't matter if God healed me or not; He was still God. For whatever reason, He allowed me to endure, to live. Tired of fighting, I totally laid my life in God's hands and made my battle His. After a hot bath, I went to bed. Like the steamy water and thick quilt, God's grace covered me, and I could breathe again. I slept for eight hours.

God, I know I died to myself out there today. It was a painful death, but a necessary one. You showed me You're in control. No matter what happens to me, I'll always remember that. Thank You, Holy One, out of the goodness of Your love, in Your great mercy, You came to me. My battle is Yours.

God, I lay my battles in Your hands:

Chapter Thirty-Eight
Fear of the Unknown

*He will have no fear of bad news; his heart is
steadfast, trusting in the Lord.*
—Psalm 112:7

The rain lasted for three days. I pulled the covers over my tired
body, glad for the third day's end. In spite of the weather and feeling so rotten, I'd hosted a cookout for a few friends. It was good to
have people over to the house, and I considered the cookout "successful." Grateful that I was to the point where food was put away
and the house was back in shape, I prayed for a good night's sleep.
Lying there, I couldn't rest; I couldn't seem to get enough air to be
comfortable.

Frightened and lonely, I sobbed as lashing rain and howling wind
beat against the house. I hugged Harm's shirt and Sis's teddy for
comfort. In the distance, the lonely sound of a train whistle intensi-
fied my longings. Fear of the unknown became my companion. It
was the longest night of my life yet.

The next morning, I called the doctor. Maybe I needed my
medication changed one more time. Since it was Sunday, my doctor told me to go to the ER, so I did. What I heard put everything
into perspective.

I was in congestive heart failure.

One of the stents placed in my artery hadn't been successful; it
had probably stopped working within days of the procedure. All the
symptoms I'd been experiencing now made sense. The damage to
my heart didn't look good. I was blessed to be alive.

*I feel like Job, God. Where does it end? I'm at Your mercy. Guard
my life. In spite of these "evil tidings" Lord, my trust is in You.*

I put my trust in You, God:

Chapter Thirty-Nine
A Deep Valley

*For he guards the course of the just and
protects the way of his faithful ones.
—Proverbs 2:8*

Seven days in the hospital felt like eternity. As my heart muscle healed, I learned that I could control my heart arrhythmia with medication. I thanked God it wasn't worse and went home with a lot of medications and a heavy heart.

The road to recovery wasn't easy. My first visit to the cardiac rehabilitation program resulted in another hospital stay. An abnormality in my EKG showed up, and my shortness of breath was back. I ended up back in the hospital with another heart catheterization. The doctors found nothing significant and adjusted medications. My problem resolved, I went home and began a slow and steady time of healing.

Jessica, my twenty-two year old granddaughter, moved in with me the day I came home from the hospital. What a blessing! A working college student, her enthusiasm for life rubbed off on me a little more each day. Each month, I healed more.

The first year anniversary of Harm's death was a milestone in my life. In his memory, the girls and I tossed mauve and crimson roses down the river and watched the flowers peacefully float away.

A knowing floated along the water: I've walked the deepest part of the valley of tears. I vowed to keep my face to the sunshine, and not focus on the shadows.

Thank you, God, for Your protection as I've walked through this deep valley. Your grace covered me as I confronted my fears. I move beyond the deep sadness now. I feel a profound shift in my grieving process. A torn place in my soul is beginning to mend. Guard my course; in You, Holy One, I move on.

Lord God, take me forward in these ways:

Chapter Forty
Everyday Normal

Be strong and take heart, all you
who hope in the Lord.
—Psalm 31:24

Life began to settle into a sense of normal with the full responsibilities of a large home. Armed with God's Word daily, I stepped into new territory.

One of the first things I tackled was changing the filters in the furnace. Looking into every nook and cranny for the dirty filters so that I could replace them, I decided their location was a well-kept secret. Plopping onto the floor, I screamed an exclamation of frustration before calling the store where we bought the furnace for instructions on what to do. I'm sure they're still laughing.

My next project was adding salt to the water softener. It sounded easy enough. Boy, was I wrong. Getting the heavy bag from the car down to the basement was more than I could handle. Placing the heavy bag on a throw rug, I pulled the monster across the tile floors, sputtering all the way. "Why did Harm make this house so long? It seems like I just passed through one Zip Code zone and am entering into another—and I'm still not to the stairs!" I thought that was bad, but getting the bag down the stairs was the really fun part.

I walked down the stairs before the bag, tugging on the plastic gently. Over the carpet it went, bouncing down step one, then step two. Then Ginger decided to help. Trying to get past the rug that the bag sat on, she lost her balance. Letting go of the bag, I caught Ginger as she went tumbling by. The salt bag rumbled and tumbled past the both of us. Hitting bottom, the bag burst, and salt flew everywhere. Together, we cleaned it up; she tracked it all over, and I followed her with the sweeper.

Eventually, the salt made it into the water softener. Later, a realization hit me: I could have driven the car around to the walk out and unloaded the unwieldy bag just feet from its destination.

The gas fireplace was an insult to my integrity. I could have stood on my head and still not been able to light the crazy thing. It upset me so much, I kicked the front of the grate—hard! That fireplace kicked back! As I sat on the floor cradling my abused foot, I remembered how many times Harm lost his cool while trying to light it. Now I understood. After hearing my story of my fight with the fireplace, a kind friend took pity on me and lit the pilot light, so all I had to do was turn a knob. I wish I could ask Harm why he never did that.

God, I think You and Harm are up there laughing at me learning to run this house—and it's not funny! Nevertheless, Holy One, with Your protection, I'll make it, and perhaps I can share my struggles with others. Help me to settle into a sense of "normal" in my everyday life.

My everyday life is "normal" in these ways:

Chapter Forty-One
Grandma is Grounded

There is a time to weep and a time to laugh.
—Ecclesiastes 3:3

Life moved on. My granddaughter Jessica brought laughter into my world again.

After Jessica lived with me a few months, she grounded me from baking. She told me the freezer was better than a bakery. Eyes flashing, she stood in front of me holding her silly, dirty stuffed lion and announced, "You're just trying to fatten me up with all your baking, Grandma! You don't want any boy to marry me! You want me to live here forever!"

"I've been found out!" I laughed. Completely dramatic, my granddaughter was a born entertainer with ideas of her own that made me smile.

Like the time she threw a stack of her dirty clothes into the dryer for fluffing. Her eyes danced. "Grandma, you don't have time to wash them." Taking her messy clothes, she put them in a heap on my bedroom floor, sprayed them with perfume, and tossed them in the dryer. Then she asked me to help her pick out an outfit to wear that evening. I stood flabbergasted as she modeled one outfit after another, looking like she had just stepped out of the dryer herself.

A new chapter began when Jessica lived with me: I began to date. One day, I found myself complaining to Jessica about a guy who wasn't good about calling me back when he said he would. Her eyes grew large. "Welcome to my world. Grandma!" she proclaimed, giving me a high-five.

That was the beginning of my asking her advice about guys. One of my girlfriends even went as far as asking Jessica for a lesson on how to flirt. Imagine us, sitting like schoolgirls, talking about flirting! With my friend engaged a month later, Jessica took full credit.

Jessica always called on my phone, and it seemed like I always ran downstairs to answer her phone. I also had to click into my call waiting—often—only to find Jessica on the line for some reason or another. It was more than a little irritating. So I decided to "get her back."

One morning, I waited until I heard Jessica taking a shower downstairs and then turned the hot water on in the other three bathrooms and the kitchen sink. Later, while Jessica walked by with a strange look on her face, I smiled and fought the urge to ask if she enjoyed her cold shower. Grandma felt much better! It was great to realize that my sense of humor and fun had returned.

I realized that laughter was playing a big part in my healing process. Laughter helped me past the weeping, past the guilt, past the feeling of being alone. I still missed Harm and mourned for him. But for the first time, I felt at peace for him and for myself.

Thank You, God, for bringing me to the place where I can laugh again. It's nice to know I can go on with my life and even date, and not feel guilty about it. I pray Jessica always remembers this special time with her grandma and know how much I love her. Help me to continue to laugh, live, and grow in You.

Thank you, God, for these
wonderful moments of laughter:

Chapter Forty-Two
Beyond Self

*The Lord will fulfill his purpose for me; your love,
O Lord, endures forever—do not abandon the
works of your hands.*
—Psalm 138:8

How could it be March? Soon it will be two years since losing my darling Harm. Within that time, my entire world has changed. In reading back through my journal, it's so clear how God has led, healed, and protected me.

I've received healing in my heart; testing shows that it's back to normal. My blood work couldn't be better, and I no longer have restrictions on what I can do. Praise God, I can get on with my life!

Snow still lies in a thin blanket on the ground. Looking out toward the river, I marveled at one of God's most enchanting winter scenes and penned its poetic vision:

Winter Enchantment
The raw beauty of the river peeks from
beneath fluffy white covers.
With subtle grace it carves a path over
rocks and logs, rushing to its destiny.
Overlapping trees intertwine into a
mass sparkle of spider webs,
Caught in its web is winter....

Over the past two years, my journal existed as a vehicle to restore wholeness in my life. I have both been blessed and challenged by using this journal. Many times I struggled, unable to write, with pain so raw, the salty taste of my tears became my only food. In those times of protest, I cried out to God, "This is too hard! I can't do it, Father!" Every time, the urge to write took me beyond myself and brought me back to Him.

We have many different journeys to make in our lives; each journey takes us down an unfamiliar path. Some disturb our comfort zone, forcing us to look beyond ourselves and to Him for direction. These are the times to look to God to hold us, to lead us, to take us through the valley of tears.

Through each journey, and in each valley, our Father God wants His very best for us. We never walk alone. God Himself walks with us. He gives us loving support and care in a gift called grace. We find God's grace in His Words—the Bible. As we read them, His hopeful words become ours. God gives us grace to endure. God gives us grace to go on. His grace covers all we go through, giving us hope and newness. In time, as we lean on His grace, we are fully restored and made whole again.

Father, after my husband's death, I thought that having a heart attack was the worst thing that could happen to me. Now I know that it wasn't, for that was the time I surrendered my entire heart to You, to take me through the valley of grief. From that time, I released the worst of the pain, and your joy began to fill my life. Now your joy spills out of my life to others. Thank You, Holy One, God who created me and loves me, for Your grace in my valley of tears.

Father, show me how You are taking me through my valley of tears:

Chapter Forty-Three
When the Heart Is Ready

*Now the God of hope fill you with all joy and peace
in believing, that you may abound in hope,
through the power of the Holy Spirit.*
—Romans 15:13

Heavenly Father,

I come to you on behalf of every person
who reads this journal. I pray You will
give them deep comfort, courage and
strength as they walk through this valley
of grief. Cover them with grace, Holy
One. Hold them steady with your love.
Thank You, God, that your love can turn
tragedy into triumph. And when their
heart is ready, Lord, take them beyond
their sorrow to the joy of saying "Yes" to
a new tomorrow.

My prayer:

Post Script
A New Journey

Be of good courage, and he shall strengthen your heart, all ye that hope in the Lord.
—Psalm 31:24

With a deep, compelling desire to reopen my heart, I take out my journal and catch you up on where God has taken me.

I stay close to God. Learning who I am without my husband is a slow and steady process. God is most gracious to me, taking me past myself into a higher place of trusting in Him. He has shown me His plan and his purpose for my life, and I'm excited to see where He leads.

I'm still living in the big house. In some ways, I don't think I'll ever get completely used to being alone.

I'm sad that Ginger no longer is with me. She died last summer. Although I only had my pet for three short years, she was a special blessing from God. Ginger filled my life with special joy.

My granddaughter Jessica is now married. She and hubby Nate have blessed me with my first great grandson. I don't believe Jessica or I will ever forget the year we lived together. It was an assignment from God. We learned from each other.

The once-groomed flower garden in the front circle now resembles a jungle (I keep waiting for a lion or a tiger to jump out!). It makes for a good conversational piece.

The critters that live in my front yard have built what resembles a city. It's filled with its own hotels, most of them higher than the Empire State Building. Not really, but I tell my friends the squirrels and rabbits and moles all needed someplace to live, and after all, I have plenty of room. Besides, it gives the dogs in the neighborhood something to chase. The bonus: My yard is fertilized for free.

As you can see, my sense of humor has fully returned. It's wonderful to laugh again, to want to live. So long as there is life in our bodies, God wants us to get up and go on. Praise God, I have been able to do that. And so will you.

I'm active in the Singles Vision program in my church. Recently, I started leading a life group that meets once a week in my home for singles ages 50+. The Lord has blessed me richly with my church family. I continually stay anchored in God's Word, never wanting to stop growing in Him.

For the last two years, copies of this journal have been passed around in manuscript form to those God brought across my path. Many letters and calls of thanks by grievers blessed with hope came my way, and the demand for copies of the book led to its publishing.

My heart cries with those who have lost a loved one. I know how it feels. I have been there. My desire is to spread hope to those hurting, to help others realize that the suffering will pass. There exists a new tomorrow, full of hope!

I am on a new journey with God, who continues to give me a bountiful harvest of joy reaped after suffering. The Lord's words in Psalm 126:5 ring in my soul: "They that sow in tears shall reap in joy."

Thank You, Holy One, that You are Worthy. My heart is full of thanksgiving and gratitude for the tranquility you have brought back into my life.

Words of Hope to Those Grieving

God sent his Son Jesus Christ into the world to give you a future and a hope. Because we're human, we aren't perfect; we fail. We need a bridge to God. We can't work our way to God; God reached out to us. He made a bridge to us through Jesus Christ. Jesus took all our failures and shortcomings on himself and died on the cross in our place, in order that we could be in right relationship with God the Father. All we have to do is accept this grace-filled gift by acknowledging that Jesus died on the cross for us, and ask Him to be the Lord, the Director, of our lives, as One who we look to for daily direction and guidance.

Jesus Christ said, "I am the resurrection and the life; he who believes in Me shall live even if he dies, and everyone who lives and believes in me shall never die." (John 11:25)

If you have not invited Jesus to be the Director of your life, and would like to, pray to Him. Ask him to show you Himself. Back in 1985, I said a prayer and gave my life to God. That prayer changed my life in great and wonderful ways. Here it is:

O God, I am a sinner; I make mistakes and fail. Please forgive me for my sins. I want to be in right relationship with You. I give my life to You right now and receive Jesus Christ as my Savior, the One who makes me right with You. I confess Him as Lord and Director of my life. From this point forward, I want to follow Him and serve Him. I want to grow and enjoy right relationship with You and others. Thank You for hearing this prayer. Thank you for changing my life right now. Amen.

If you prayed this prayer and deeply meant it within your heart, then you've begun a "new life" in right relationship with God. As one who follows Christ, a Christian, your life is changed for eternity. God is great and awesome, and He will direct and guide your life.

The poem read at Harm's celebration of life:

From a Loved One in Heaven

I would not have you grieve for me today
Nor weep beside my vacant chair.
Could you but know my daily portion here
You would not, could not, wish me there.

I know now why He said, "Ear hath not heard"
I have no words, no alphabet.
Or even if I had I dare not tell
Because you could not bear it yet.

So, only this—I am the same, though changed
Like Him! A joy more rich and strong
than I had dreamed that any heart could hold
And all my life is one glad song.

Sometimes when you are talking to our Lord
He turns and speaks to me…Dear heart,
In that rare moment you and I are just
the distance of a word apart!

And so my loved ones, do not grieve for me
Around the family board today;
Instead, rejoice, for we are one in Him,

And so I am not far away.
—Martha Snell Nicholson

"To depart and be with Christ which is far better."
—Philippians 1:23